KUDOS for Pascha Press

"The author does a wonderful job in offering kind and comforting words for inquisitive children."

    -On *When My Baba Died*, Presvytera Vassi Haros, *Orthodox Christian Network*

"This beautifully written book, filled with wonderful photos, is an important aid for those who wish to help a child understand death, and loss. I highly recommend it for every church bookstore, and every home library."

    -On *When My Yiayia Died*, Abbot Tryphon, creator of *The Morning Offering* blog on Ancient Faith and rector of All-Merciful Savior Monastery, Vashon Island, WA

When Mama Had Cancer

When Mama Had Cancer

Marjorie Kunch

Foreword by Father Joseph Gleason

O Lord, how manifold are Thy works!
In wisdom hast Thou made them all...

Psalm 104:24 as found on the South Rim at the Grand Canyon

PASCHA PRESS

Educate Edify Entertain

Copyright © 2017 Marjorie Kunch

All rights reserved. No part of this publication may be reproduced or transmitted in any form or by any means electronic or mechanical, including photocopy, recording, or any storage and retrieval system now known or to be invented without prior written permission from the publisher or author.

Pascha Press
mkunch@paschapress.com
Toll-free telephone: 1-844- 4-PASCHA
http://www.paschapress.com

This publication is designed to provide accurate information, for general purposes only, in regard to the subject matter covered. There are no warranties or representations, expressed or implied. It is sold with the understanding that the publisher and author are not engaged in rendering legal, medical, spiritual, or other professional advice. If expert assistance is required by the reader, the services of a competent professional person in your area should be sought. Before following suggestions found in a book, magazine, website, chat room, group, or any other source, always check with your physician first.

ISBN 978-0- 9964045-5- 6

Dedicated to my Pink Sisters who taught me how to fight like a girl, and to my brothers and sisters in Christ from the group *Orthodox Christians Fight Cancer*.

Thank you to the wonderful staff at MD Anderson Cancer Center, my oncologist Dr. Theresa Liu-Dumlao, surgeon Dr. Julie Billar, the Gleason and Lucovich families, and Father Thomas Frisby.

Thank you to my family and friends who helped us through this trial by watching the children so I could attend myriad doctor appointments; thanks to those who brought or arranged for meals, sent cards and gifts, wrote letters and emails, visited our home, and prayed for my health - I love you all more than you will ever know.

Thank you to James for your inspiring words and my undying gratitude to Jen and Lori for turning what would have been one of the saddest days of my life into one full of belly laughs.

I deeply appreciate the Facebook fans of Pascha Press who helped cover my medical expenses through donations to my Youcaring campaign.

Special acknowledgment of my devoted husband Christopher who stood by my side in sickness and in health, my children Mattias and Everilde, and goddaughter Xenia who gave this Mama a reason to stay the course and finish the race.

Thanks be to God for giving us the Word to be comforted with, the Theotokos, and the intercessory prayers of St. John Maximovitch the Wonderworker of San Francisco, St. Nektarios, and St. Panteleimon for my healing.

Credits

Images: Christopher Kunch and Marjorie Kunch
Software: Fotosketcher.com

Book Design: Kristina Tartara, www.kristinatartara.com

Shot on location in Gilbert, Safford, and Jerome, AZ; and Glasgow, Scotland

MD Anderson Cancer Center
2946 E. Banner Gateway Drive
Gilbert, AZ 85234

St. Gabriel Orthodox Church
77 Southpark Ave
Glasgow, G12 8LE, UK

Barbifer
140 Main Street
Jerome, AZ 86331

St. Paisius Monastery
10250 Sky Blue Rd.
Safford, AZ 85546

Bible quotes KJV, clip art, and stock photography sourced from the public domain

Microscope: Amazon
Cell division: Cancer Research UK
Doctors: iStock
Monastics: Father Michael Wood and Sister Margaret Smythe of St. Bride Hermitage, Scotland

Foreword

As a father of eight children, I welcome the publication of this new book, *When Mama Had Cancer*. I recommend this book for both family libraries and church libraries. When I had my own battle with cancer, I wish this book had been available for my children to read.

Cancer is a difficult topic, especially for children. It is scary enough for the adults to deal with, even when they understand what is happening. It can be even scarier for young children who are bewildered, having no idea what is going on.

Why is Mama so sick all the time? Why doesn't she get better? Why is her hair falling out? Is Mama going to be OK? Why did God let this happen? There are so many questions, and it can be difficult to answer them in a way that makes sense to a child. So when a family member is diagnosed with cancer, how can we help our children understand?

Marjorie's new book, *When Mama Had Cancer*, helps children see cancer from a Christian perspective. Her book explains what cancer is, what symptoms to expect, and what children can do to help. Explanations are given in a simple way, helping to make cancer less mysterious, and less scary to deal with.

More importantly, this book points children towards Christ. We are reminded that God has not forgotten us, and that cancer is not a reason for despair. During times of sickness, we are encouraged to trust in the love of God, the support of the Church, and the power of prayer.

Marjorie has the life experience necessary to write this book, because she personally fought cancer herself. Throughout the ordeal, she helped her young children understand what was going on, and she taught them how to trust in Christ throughout it all. She gives a wonderful gift to the rest of us, by providing us with a children's book that can help families deal with this subject in a truly Christian way. Thank you, Marjorie!

-Fr. Joseph Gleason
Rostov Veliky, Russia

One spring day, I was playing with my sister and we heard the phone ring. Mama looked worried. She said this was an important call about her test results and left the room. I heard Mama say she will go to the doctor's office tomorrow to discuss her treatment plan and then she began to cry.

Sometimes adults get scared and cry when they hear bad news. This made us very sad and we felt a little scared, too. These are normal emotions no matter what your age may be. The good news is that we can ask God to help us be brave during scary times.

"Be of good courage, and He shall strengthen your heart, all ye that hope in the Lord."

- Psalm 31:24

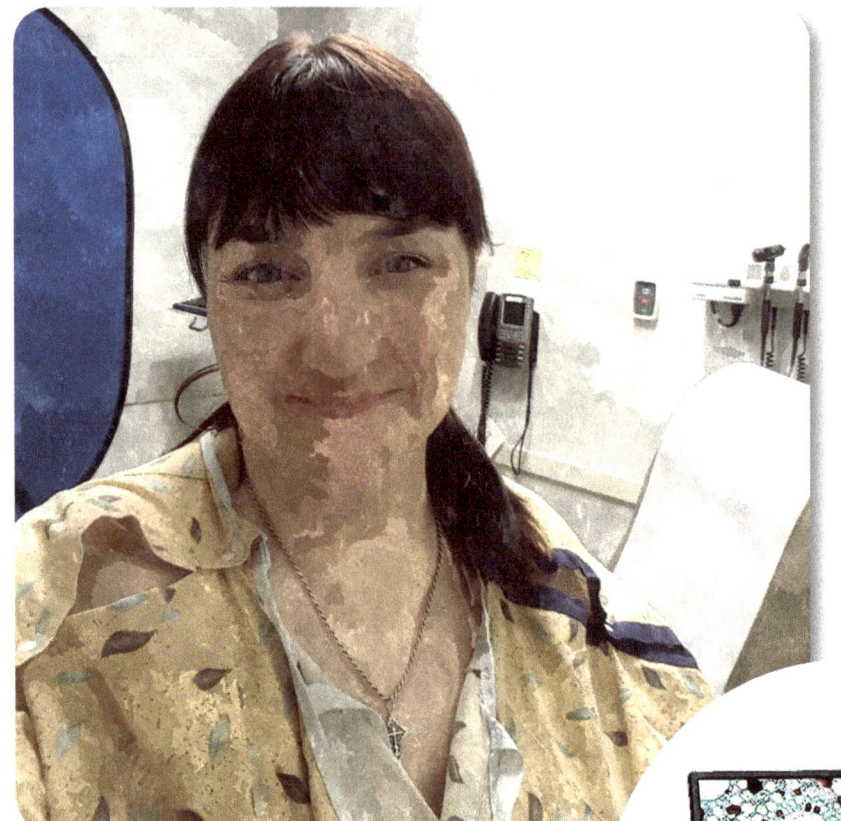

I remember Mama telling Papa she felt a lump. She then had to go to the doctor's office to see what it might be. They took a picture of the inside of her body.

She next needed to have a test called a **biopsy**. This is when the doctor makes a tiny cut called an incision near the suspicious area. They took out some tissue and viewed it under a microscope. Doctors then determined if the cells were benign, which means not harmful, or malignant, another way to say cancerous. The incision was so small Mama did not need stitches afterwards, just an ice pack and a bandage like I get when I scrape my knee.

Papa came home early from work the day of the phone call. He asked us all to come sit by Mama on the sofa and give her a big hug. Papa told us that the test showed Mama had **cancer**. She will be sick for several months while she goes through treatments to get rid of the **tumor** the doctors found in Mama's body.

Cancer Arises When Cells Divide Out of Control

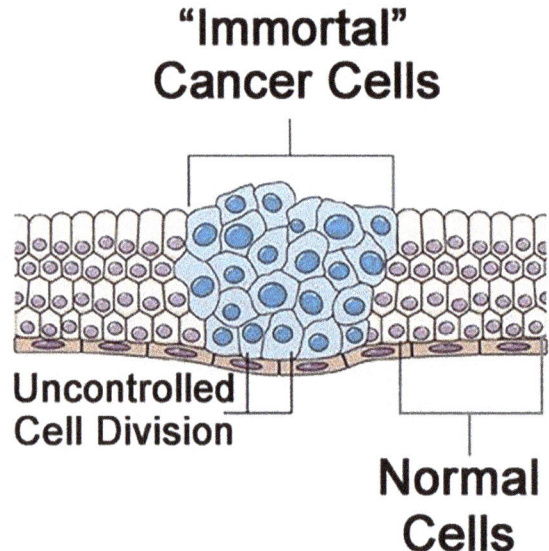

What is cancer, anyway? Papa explained that cancer is made up of cells in someone's body that grow very fast and this is not normal. Normal cells grow, divide, know when to stop growing, and eventually die. They are then replaced with new cells so the tissues in our body stay healthy.

A cancer cell does not work normally; they continue to grow and divide out of control and don't die like they are supposed to, causing disease.

A cancerous tumor is a lump of cells that damage the body's healthy cells and tissue. This can make someone very sick. We did not have to worry about catching cancer from Mama like how someone catches a cold. That is not how this disease works, it is not spread from person to person but instead is caused by a ***gene mutation***.

Mama can't make us sick so we could kiss and hug her lots! Mama needed lots of love in the days following her diagnosis.

Let's meet some of the people who helped Mama through her cancer.

There are special doctors who focus only on treating tumors and they are called oncologists. An **oncologist** has spent many years studying and researching this disease. They are specialists, another way of saying experts, on cancer. It is their job to try to cure people of this sickness, or at least bring people into remission. This means to either reduce or take away completely the symptoms of cancer, even if some of the sick cells remain.

Oncologists will do everything they can with these goals in mind. They will use many tools, such as taking pictures of the inside of a person's body with an **MRI** machine, use **chemotherapy**, apply **radiation**, and recommend **surgery**.

There were nurses who helped Mama by giving her the medicines the doctors prescribed, and even the nurses had helpers who brought Mama food and warm blankets during her treatments.

Mama's cancer center had volunteers who came around with special carts to give patients comfort items like lotion, lip balm, fuzzy socks, hats, and even candy! There are many helpers in the medical world for people with cancer.

Did you know that there are even helpers specifically for Orthodox Christians? Let's learn about them!

Is any among you afflicted? Let him pray.

Is any merry? Let him sing psalms.

Is any sick among you? Let him call for the elders of the church and let them pray over him, anointing him with oil in the name of the Lord.

James 5:13-14

We prayed as a family in our *icon corner*. We asked special saints known for helping people with cancer - such as Saint John the Wonderworker of Shanghai and San Francisco, Saint Luke the physician, and Saint Nektarios - to intercede on our behalf. We asked them to pray to God for Mama since they stand before His throne in heaven.

Medicine is good for our bodies and prayer is good for our souls. There were lots of helpers who prayed to God for my family at church and this made me feel better. Some people sent beautiful cards and care packages to help Mama feel better. Friends also stopped by to visit or bring us a yummy meal. Can you think of other things people can do to help someone when they have cancer?

Mama has friends all over the world! She met them online in support groups for Orthodox Christians with cancer. They had lots of suggestions, for example they told Mama to obtain a copy of the icon of the Theotokos named *Panagia Pantanassa*, which is known for helping people with cancer. They lit candles and prayed for our family at their churches, and some even sent very special oil that came from the **lampadas** that burn before the **relics** of saints.

Mama was given oil from Kazan in Russia, San Francisco and Platina in California, and Mount Athos in Greece. *Kardiotisa* is another miracle-working icon of the Mother of God, located in Pennsylvania, which streams **myrrh**. Someone from her group sent her a cotton swab of this holy substance.

Before Mama began her treatments, she visited a special place called a ***monastery.*** She asked the ***monastics*** who live there to pray a special service for her called a ***Moleben.***

Have you ever met a monk or nun before? They are special people chosen by God who pray for everyone morning, noon, and night. Mama was able to attend Divine Liturgy every day at the monastery, she did not have to wait until Sunday! Isn't that wonderful?

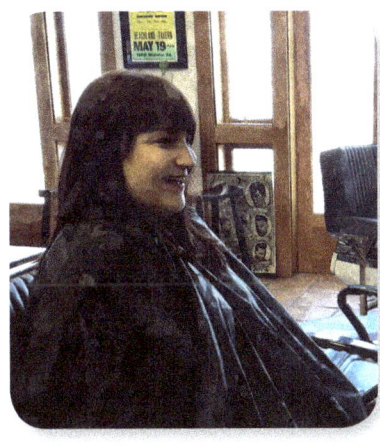  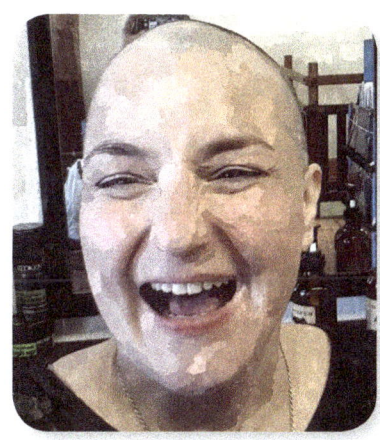

When Mama returned from the monastery she went to a barber shop to shave her head. The chemotherapy she had to take would make her hair all fall out anyway, so she wanted it to come off on her terms. Mama was temporarily bald for a short time. She joked and said having no hair was cooler for the summer.

Although she looked very different, she was still our Mama and always will be.

Sissy loved to pat Mama's soft, fuzzy head. This made Mama laugh! It's only hair after all, it grows back.

"A merry heart doeth good like a medicine."   - Proverbs 17:22

The week after her barber trip, Mama began her chemotherapy sessions. This is extraordinarily strong medicine given at a hospital to kill cancer cells.

Unfortunately, this medicine also has strong side effects as it kills some healthy cells, too. This is why her hair would have fallen out in big messy clumps if she had not shaved it.

Mama had a **port** inserted into her chest, this is how she received her IV medications without getting poked in the arm all the time.

We talked a lot about ways to help Mama during this time, and we also talked about when this extra help would not be needed because chemotherapy does eventually end. We marked her last chemotherapy treatment on a calendar and counted the days.

You should also ask your loved one to show you on a calendar when their last chemotherapy session will be. Maybe plan a special party to celebrate reaching this milestone!

Mama temporarily could not eat like she used to, as the taste buds on her tongue died due to the chemotherapy. She was very tired after her treatments and took lots of naps. I was a helper when I brought Mama applesauce to eat when she had to stay in bed. My sister and I quietly read a book when Mama needed to sleep.

The chemotherapy also made Mama's tummy very upset. Sometimes I even heard her spit up.

*"For I was hungry and you gave Me food;
I was thirsty and you gave Me drink."* - Matthew 25:35

This was scary but I knew what to do. I brought Mama some water and asked if I needed to call Papa at work.

We practiced how to dial the telephone and we taped his phone number to the wall so I could always find it. If an emergency occurred, for example Mama could not wake up or breathe, I knew to call 9-1-1.

I ended up not ever needing to call an ambulance for Mama, but it made me feel safe to know what to do in any and all situations.

Rejoice, the Medicine that reduces pain!

Rejoice, the Coolness that cools fever of the ailments!

Rejoice, you who cauterize the illness of cancer like fire!

Akathist of the Mother of God,
Pantanassa, Healer of Cancer

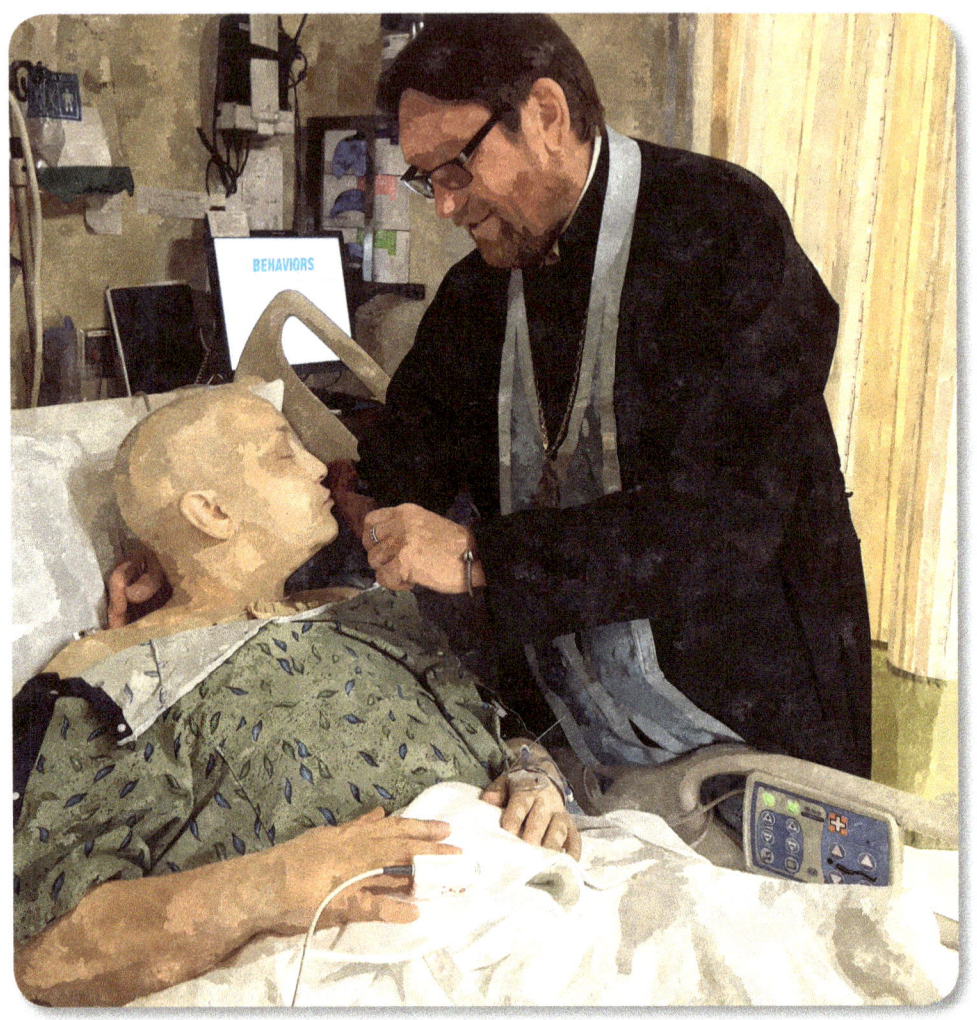

Although Mama's chemotherapy ended that autumn, she next needed to have surgery. Our priest came to the hospital to pray for a successful surgery that will remove all of the diseased tissue the cancer caused. He brought her the cross to **venerate** and anointed her with **holy oil.**

My sister and I then went to play at our cousin's house while Papa stayed at the hospital to wait for the surgeon to finish, as this procedure takes several hours. When Mama was all done, she was very tired and sore but she was okay! She had to spend the night at the hospital.

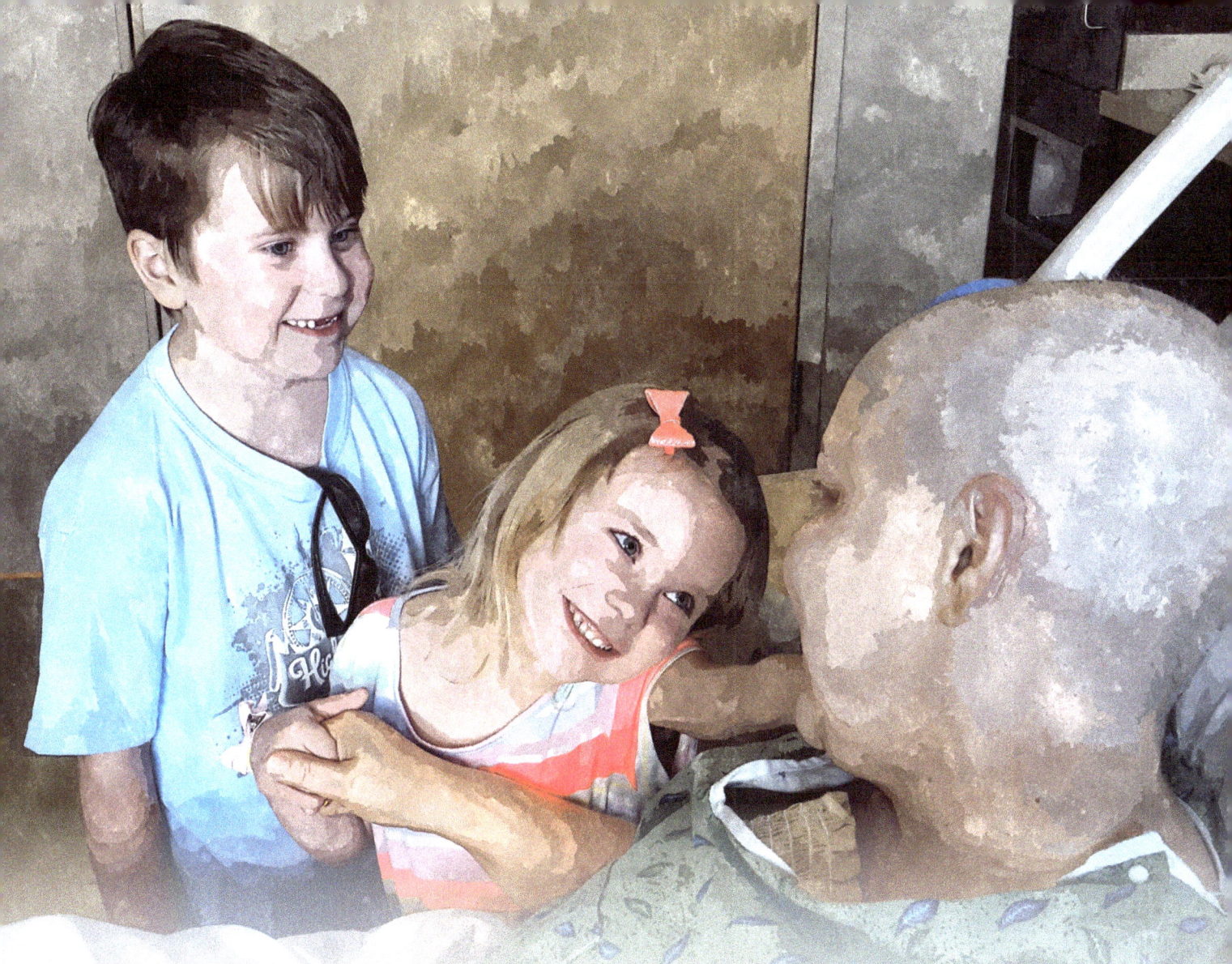

We were so excited to get to the hospital the next day to bring Mama home! My sister and I drew her pictures of hearts to let her know how much we love her! We had to be careful to not jump on Mama or hug her too tight. She had stitches to heal and also little tubes attached to a bag, called a **JP drain.** When a few weeks passed Mama had these drains removed. We helped Mama do her exercises so she could continue to heal well and get stronger.

Sometimes, just sometimes, although a person prayed, completed all of their treatments, had Holy Unction, had surgery, and did everything the doctors and priests said to do, their cancer does not go away. Sometimes a person will pass away because of this disease.

This will not be their fault, your fault, the doctor's fault, the priest's fault, or even God's fault, although you may feel that way. Sickness is not a curse from God, but like all bad things it is the result of living in a fallen world. We are sad for the loss of our loved one, as well as for the loss of being able to live in an earthly paradise. It is healthy for us to talk about our feelings of ***grief*** with a trusted helper.

Do not grieve endlessly, for there is hope! Remember the joy of Pascha, Christ trampled down death by death to make a way for us to again enter paradise. To die is to have God call people home to Him where there is no more sickness or suffering. It is simply their time to join the Heavenly Kingdom.

Remember that because we are Orthodox Christians, we will always be connected to our deceased loved ones through the Holy Church. We will remember them on **Soul Saturdays.** We can hold ***Mnimosino*** or ***Panikhida*** services in their memory. They will remain a part of our family forever.

It was hard for me to not be afraid. I was anxious that Mama might not get better, but she said her type of cancer was caught early and she only had a 10% chance of it coming back. This meant she had a 90% chance of staying healthy, so I did my best to not worry.

Papa said if these fears do not go away, I could talk to our priest about it and he will teach me ways to combat these thoughts. I also read comforting verses in the Bible and recited the Jesus Prayer. My example helped Sissy not be afraid, too.

At church we lit candles and said a prayer for all of the people who are fighting cancer. This made us feel better since we helped out in such an important way.

Week by week, Mama began to look and act like herself again and we were so thankful to God for her healing. By the following spring Mama no longer needed to take naps. She chased us around on the playground again, like she used to before her illness. Her hair eventually grew back. There was a new normal in our lives, we appreciated our time together more than ever before. We took walks to watch the stars rise in the evening. We turned off the TV to sit outside and listen to the birds sing in the sunshine. Mama and Papa surprised us with mid-week trips for an ice cream cone. We didn't take the simple joys in life for granted anymore.

Mama's cancer journey was almost complete. She had to have frequent check-ups for a few years, but the doctors said they are confident she will remain healthy. We will continue to pray this remains true.

During that season of our lives, my sister and I learned that cancer patients have so many helpers. We learned people really do live the commandment to love one another. All around the world there are people who care about my family. There are people who care about your family, too. People on earth and in heaven, everywhere! You are not alone.

When Mama had cancer, we were scared at first, but as she got stronger so did our family and faith. We learned how to rely on God and how to let others bless us, too. We learned about grace and humility. We worked together and helped Mama triumph over cancer. I learned that Sissy was a helper by bringing Mama blankets when she was cold, I brought her water when she was thirsty, and we prayed for her just like Jesus said we should. Even though my sister and I were small, we were helpers just as important as the grown-ups, doctors, and nurses.

It is so special that we Orthodox Christians have many helpers in our time of need: God, Jesus, the Holy Spirit, a multitude of saints, family, church members, and friends.

Can you be a helper for your loved one, too?

"Sickness is a blessing for man in the sense that, if one uses it appropriately, one can draw from it considerable spiritual benefit, thereby making what was originally a sign of mortality into an instrument of salvation."

-St. John Chrysostom

Glossary of Terms

Biopsy- Tissue removed and examined under a microscope to discover the presence or extent of a suspected disease.

Cancer- A disease or tumor caused by the uncontrolled division of abnormal cells in a part of the body.

Chemotherapy- The use of chemical substances to treat cancer at the cellular level.

Gene Mutation- A permanent alteration in the DNA sequence of your genetic make-up. It is not known for sure what causes these changes, some scientists think environmental factors play a part.

Grief- The normal process of reacting to a profound loss; a feeling of deep sorrow.

Holy Oil- The portion of olive oil that was blessed by a priest when celebrating Holy Unction for the sick.

Icon Corner- A small worship space created in the homes of Orthodox Christians for prayer.

JP Drain- A closed-suction medical device of plastic tubes and bulbs that is commonly used after surgery to allow bodily fluids to drain away, preventing swelling and infection.

Lampada- The oil lamp that is typically hung before a sacred object such as an icon or reliquary.

Moleben- A Slavic prayer service where one asks for supplication or intercession in a particular matter done in honor of Christ, the Theotokos, or a particular saint. Related to a Paraklesis service.

Mnimosino- The "Calling to Mind" service done in remembrance of an Orthodox loved one who has fallen asleep in the Lord.

Monastery- A community of monastics who live together bound under religious vows.

Monastic- A man (monk) or woman (nun) who has dedicated their lives to God by remaining in a constant state of prayer.

MRI- A magnetic resonance imaging machine that creates detailed images of the organs and tissues found within your body.

Myrrh- A fragrant gum or resin typically found in certain trees but sometimes spontaneously appears from holy objects.

Oncologist- A medical doctor who specializes in the diagnosis and treatment of tumors.

Panikhida- A memorial service chanted for the repose of the deceased. Also called a Parastos, Pomen, or Trisagion.

Port- A small medical device implanted beneath the skin where a catheter connects it to a vein in order to administer IV medications.

Radiation- The treatment of disease using X-ray or similar forms of intense energy radiation to destroy cancerous cells.

Relics- A part of a deceased holy person's body or belongings kept as an object of reverence, not worship, as worship belongs to God alone.

Soul Saturday- Days set aside for commemoration of the dead within the liturgical year of the Eastern Orthodox Church.

Surgery- The treatment of injuries or disorders of the body by incision and removal or manipulation.

Tumor- A swelling of the part of your body caused by an abnormal growth of cells, sometimes benign or sometimes malignant.

Venerate- To regard with high respect. To respectfully bow, make the sign of the cross, and kiss a holy object as a sign of piety and devotion.

Resources

The Akathist to the Mother of God "Healer of Cancer" can be ordered from:

St. Paisius Serbian Orthodox Monastery
PO Box 1075
10250 Sky Blue Rd.
Safford, AZ 85548
www.stpaisiusmonastery.org

The myrrh streaming icon of the Theotokos can be visited at:

St. George Orthodox Church
743 S. Keyser Ave.
Taylor, PA 18517
www.stgeorgestaylor.com

Holy Oil of St. John Maximovitch and Molebens can be requested from:

Holy Virgin Cathedral
6210 Geary Blvd.
San Francisco, CA 94121
www.sfsobor.com

Holy Oil of Blessed Fr. Seraphim Rose can be requested from:

St. Herman of Alaska Monastery
10 Beegum Gorge Rd.
Platina, CA 96076
www.sainthermanmonastery.org

Saints for Special Intentions Associated with Cancer:

St. Agatha of Sicily
Anargyri (Sts. Cosmas and Damian)
Archangel Raphael
St. Gabriel Urgebadze of Mtskheta
St. John Maximovitch the Wonderworker
St. Luke the Surgeon of Simferopol and Crimea
St. Nektarios of Aegina
St. Panteleimon

By no means an exhaustive list, just a few select websites one can visit to obtain more information about their particular cancer and where various resources can be found to put you in touch with the various helpers that exist:

American Cancer Society: www.cancer.org

Cancer Care, support groups and information: www.cancercare.org

Also can find here links for children with parents who have cancer: www.cancercare.org/tagged/children

Cancer Horizons, free headcoverings: www.cancerhorizons.com/free-stuff/hats-scarves/

National Cancer Institute: www.cancer.gov

Phil's Friends, free chemo care packages: philsfriends.org

Search Facebook to join: *Orthodox Christians Fight Cancer*

Helpful Verses in the KJV Bible

Deuteronomy 31:6	Matthew 11:28-29
Isaiah 41:10	John 14:1-3
Psalms 34:19	Romans 8:16-17, 28, 38-39
Psalms 62:6-8	2 Corinthians 1:3-4
Psalms 103:2-4	Philippians 4:6-7
Isaiah 58:8-9	1 Peter 1:21
Jeremiah 29:11	1 Peter 5:6-7

Fr. Joseph Gleason was a Calvinist and conservative Anglican. But as Fr. Joseph studied Church history, learned more about the development and canonization of Holy Scripture, and even delved into the details of Church history and the Ecumenical Councils, it was to Constantinople—and not Rome—that Fr. Joseph found he looked. After a long period of prayer, discussions, and even debates, he led a little Anglican parish in Omaha, Illinois to join the Orthodox Church. Fr. Joseph lovingly pastored as deacon for two years and as priest for another two years. In January 2017, Fr. Joseph and his family set out on a new adventure and moved to Rostov the Great, a beautiful city in Russia.

www.rostov-the- great.com
www.youcaring.com/frjosephgleason-785449

Marjorie Kunch is a mother, mortician, and Orthodox Christian who traded the snowy Midwest for the sunny Southwest. Marjorie and her husband converted to Orthodoxy on Holy Saturday, 2005. She graduated Magna Cum Laude from Worsham College of Mortuary Science and currently serves her community as a Certified Funeral Celebrant. When not writing, she is homeschooling, baking, or fangirling. Diagnosed with Stage 3b breast cancer in 2017, she asks your prayers for all who endure this affliction. No matter what, Philippians 1:21.

www.youcaring.com/marjoriekunch-770987

ALSO AVAILABLE FROM PASCHA PRESS

When My Baba Died- A gentle story that beautifully explains the Orthodox funeral service to children with special emphasis on Slavic customs and heritage.

When My Baba My Yiayia Died Activity Workbook-The perfect accompaniment to either storybook. Useful for grieving families to complete together or as a tool in the classroom to discuss death and the Orthodox response to it.

When My Yiayia Died- A gentle story that beautifully explains the Orthodox funeral service to children with special emphasis on Greek customs and heritage.

Find these titles on Amazon, Barnes and Noble, Walmart, and other retailers. Contact the publisher directly for bookstore wholesale terms or quantity purchases. Follow Pascha Press on Facebook for updates and more!

Notes

www.ingramcontent.com/pod-product-compliance
Lightning Source LLC
Chambersburg PA
CBHW061931290426
44113CB00024B/2875